The Life-Changing Art of Cleaning and Organization.

Live A Healthier Life

By: Carol Milligan Babson

I0159442

Copyright

Table Of Contents

Accomplishments

Introduction

Several years back while working as a full-time nurse pulling 8-hour and sometimes 12-hour shifts, I focused on patient care, deadlines, timeframes, and the stress that goes along with holding down a full-time job. While…my priorities were my family, and trying to keep the bills paid.
All of a sudden my life changed drastically within a matter of months. My husband became sick and had to go on disability, I was trying to cope with a back injury, and my mother needed around the clock special care, so she moved in with us.
At this time, an increase of personal belongings became an issue

that started getting out of hand. I
guess you can say we were pack rats
and we liked to nest objects for
comfort. But, more space was
needed so we had to find a way to
make a change. The most difficult
step in this process was letting go of
a few sentimental items. So taking
pictures of those objects helped me
get the job accomplished.

Chapter One: The Effects of Accumulated Clutter

The simplest road to freedom is an uncluttered one, which I have found to be true.

The more material possessions we have, the more complicated our lives get. Accumulating articles can drain our finances, rob our attention, our effort, and our time.

Just think about it, the more we own, the more time it takes to clean, maintain, organize and arrange them in a suitable location.

It seems that landfills are springing up everywhere.

Many homes are overfilled with an

excess of stuff.

Technology, marketing, work, and entertainment is distracting us from the very things that should matter the most, like a healthy less stressful life, and relationships with family and friends.

Is a sale really a sale if you do not need the item, or a bargain really a bargain if we have nowhere to display or store it.

Then we have to deal with the guilt of spending money on all these purchased items that take up unnecessary space, my bank account was bleeding massively.

Ads and commercials give us the feeling that our life would be better if we purchased their products, from an excessive amount of clothes, jewelry, exercise machines, etc. Marketers get paid to sell stuff, some items you might actually need but advertisers prey on your wallet.

Stop the guilt and move on.

Do you feel tired, stressed, and claustrophobic in your own home? Look at all the dusty knick-knacks sitting around. Dust, rodents, and insects seem to be attracted to clutter.

There is a difference between accumulating stuff and creating a life. Clutter creates tension, stress, depression, and embarrassment. Reward yourself from time to time, with the money you save.

Chapter Two: Things To Consider

Do you feel overwhelmed by the total volume of your material possessions, or are you getting complaints from family members?

Are the clothes in your closets bulging, and it's hard to find that one outfit to wear that you are searching for when you are in a hurry?

Do you feel confused and indecisive about what to do with all of this stuff, and are you attached to things you know you don't really need?

Selling versus Donating: Selling

your possessions can add extra income, but there is no guarantee that your articles will be purchased. Also, you need to be aware that it's unlikely that you will get back the full face value.

Donating things will be easier since different people will receive the objects, and hopefully your donations will be put to good use. You might want to reward a friend with something they have admired, and make them happy.

Spending money on pointless junk often means and increase in debt or not having enough money for the truly important things in life.

The concept of Feng Shui tells us that open areas have more…flow. This flow gives you energy,

abundance, and happiness in the home.
It increases confidence, when you live in a clean well-organized home, you feel a sense of pride, and a sense of control from mastering your personal space.

Chapter Three: Think About Eliminating Clutter

Typically, after the alarm clock rings in the morning, we scurry around to get dressed and/or ready for work, then parents are encouraging their kids to get to school on time.

Even if we do not have young children at home, we usually have daily activities and deadlines we need to meet.

Think about freeing your mind and living with emotional simplicity. Imagine being able to relax more and to live in a serene, nurturing, welcoming environment, with less stress and worry.

Slowly but surely, organizing and cleaning in short intervals can make life less stressful.

Everything needs to have a home of its own, clutter piles up because we don't know where to put it.

Everything needs to have a purpose in our life, whether it's beauty, joy, or it is a useful object.

Do we keep things because they were a gift, or because they were expensive? Everything we keep should be in a good working order.

If it's broken, let it go. Ask yourself, "Will it benefit me, and do I really need it?"

Set a goal of a few minutes each day to clean a particular area in your home or office. Small actions can make a massive change.

You can't solve all your problem

this week, but you can definitely gain a tiny victory over one problem area.

Examples: You may clean up a stack of papers that has been lying around, one closet, one room in your house, one drawer or one bookshelf. You get the idea.

Look at your belongings in a different way. Don't be chained any longer.

Does your stuff have a hold on you? Do you feel trapped?

Make your home feel lighter, fresher, and cleaner feeling.

Everything in your home should have a home of its own, if it gets out of place, return it to that home ASAP.

Your home will be better organized. The high we get from purchasing new items is usually short-lived.

Living large is not necessarily

living well.

Chapter Four: Getting Organized and Prepared

Prepare your mind to let some things go.

Keep your family involved with the process, and let them make some decisions.

Reserve a designated time each day to de-clutter, then organize, and lastly give that area a good cleaning.

Make ready your supplies, such as boxes, storage bins, containers with labels, or see-through containers, they are great for viewing the contents within.

Prepare a space to set your boxes or containers so you can start de-cluttering.

Sometimes taking a photo before and after a cleaning job will give you the incentive to keep up the good work.

Remove and put away items that belong in other rooms.

Clean all flat surfaces like countertops.

Keep the items that are currently useful, and in good working order, also the things you absolutely love and want to display.

Items that you don't use, or don't like, consider selling, donating, or giving them away.

If you feel obligated to keep an item because it was expensive or it was a gift, think about taking a picture of it for memories, then decide what you would like to do with that object.

Remove any furniture that is not working for your space.

Have separate boxes to put items in to sell, or to donate.
You might even need a separate container so you can organize your paperwork, like a filing system.
Remember, you can use a calendar to mark important dates on.
You may want to give some items to friends or family.
Giving freely feels good
. You'll make a friend smile, and

free up some space in your home or on a shelf.

Chapter Five: The Benefits of an Organized Home

Organizing and decluttering can reduce spending, and it helps the environment.

Some of the basic things that make life worth living are family, friends, and a home cooked meal.

Set realistic goals and incorporate discipline.

You will most likely feel healthier and more energetic by setting priorities and boundaries.

Rediscover your passions and the confidence to pursue them.

Feel less stressed, sleep more, and restore your passion for life.

Knowing your home is neat and clean, allows you to easily invite friends and coworkers to visit without worrying about what they will think.

What are some of the benefits of de-cluttering your surroundings?

You have more time for yourself.

You gain more discipline.

You gain more open space.

You have a feeling of accomplishment.

You feel more productive.

You save more money.

You gain a sense of happiness.

Improved health benefits from a cleaner home, and less stress.

Reduced injuries, you are in control of your surroundings.

Happier relationships with family and friends.

Chapter Six: Helpful Hints About De-Cluttering and Cleaning

It's better to de-clutter an area first then go back and clean it, this will save you time and energy.
Starting small is the first step to keeping you from becoming frustrated.
Day by day chip away at excess clutter.
This can be made simpler by choosing a specified time each day.
When de-cluttering ask yourself these three questions:
Do you like it?
Do you use it?
Do you need it?
If, "No" is your answer, consider

selling it, giving it away or donating it to a worthy cause.

An excess of clutter will never make you happy.

When you keep only the stuff you really need, you develop and increased appreciation for specific items and their impact on your life.

You will also focus more on the non-material pleasures of life and your gratitude for people, experiences, and nature.

You will discover what is imperative.

Some items are useful and necessary.

Some might even bring you pleasure, comfort, and fond memories.

But…more than likely a lot of stuff is clutter, like items that are disorganized, misplaced or basically no longer needed.

Your home is a reflection of you, send a message that you have your act together by keeping it clean and well organized.

Simply removing excess decorations or knick-knacks can help make a room look more inviting. Any furnishings that makes a room less functional consider selling or donating.

Sometimes, just removing a few things or changing the arrangement of others, can quickly provide you with a positive and rewarding results.

Kitchen counters is a great place to start, leave out only the appliances that you use at least three times a week.

Your kitchen counters will have more of an eye-appeal and you will feel the joy of a clean workspace.

Kitchen drawers might be a little more challenging, do you have an excess of like items such as cooking utensils, knives, and silverware, etc.?

When cleaning your refrigerator and pantry check expiration dates and discard expired foods.

Arranging similar articles together helps you to locate the item when needed.

You might want to invest in airtight containers in which to store grains, cereal, and perishable items.

When cleaning kitchen cupboards, check for cracked or chipped dishes, drinking cups, and glasses.

Bills and paperwork tend to accumulate, you may need a filing system for bills, and tax papers.

Immediate recycle or throw away any paperwork you no longer need.

You can use your home calendar to mark important dates on when sorting through your mail.
Try to keep your dining table an office space clean and appealing.
Remember to take small steps in achieving your goals.
If you became frustrated step away and take a break.
"Remember, clutter builds up over time, so don't expect to get rid of it overnight.
Try to make your bed daily, you want an inviting place to sleep.
Make sure you hang up your clothes or put them in a hamper to be laundered if soiled.
Dust your bedroom furniture.
No matter what room you are cleaning, always check your ceilings, and rid them of any cobwebs.
Don't forget to clean ceiling fans

since they are usually a big source of accumulated dust.

Linen closets might become multi-purpose closets if space is limited.

De-clutter and organize your bathroom.

If you have five or more lotions, consider leaving two of them out, so you can have an option of with one to choose from.

Check your makeup and mascara, replace these often.

Do you have an excess of clothes in your closet, and most of them you do not wear?

Consider doing the Clothes Hanger Challenge.

Make sure all your garments are turned one way on your hangers.

After you wear, an article of clothing hang it back up, but place the hook in the opposite direction. After three months any clothes you did not wear, consider selling, donating, or giving them away.

You may want to keep your grooming items in a basket or on a shelf.

Try to keep all like items together such as fingernail polish, nail files, and nail clippers.

Take small steps de-cluttering your home, one room at the time, then organize and clean.

Each step you take is progress you have made.

Chapter Seven: Look At Your Accomplishments

Feel the joy and pride after each accomplishment.
Don't be hard on yourself, maybe it took years for all of that clutter to pile up, it's called living.
De-cluttering gives you renewed energy, inner peace, and more pleasure.
Enjoy the meaningful aspects of your life.
You'll feel more confident and in control.
It seems as if we've been taught that the more stuff we have…equals greater happiness, but then we find ourselves feeling caged in and suffocating.

With a clean house, we now have more freedom, which leads to greater peace of mind.

There is happiness in having less clutter around us, less stress, less cleaning, less dust, a more open space which allows for better air circulation and natural light.

We may never be able to get rid of all the stress in our life, but if we can lessen it, we will be better off. The definition for stress: Stress is when a person's mental and emotional state is in tension, that results from the demanding situations that a person is put through.

In the future ask yourself, will this item fill your home for no reason at all, or do you really need it?

Think of taking control of your living space like a well-exercised body.

While cleaning your home, your body is in motion…exercising, and at the same time you are helping to decrease dust, airborne viruses and possibly you could be cleaning up a likely fire hazard.

It will take some effort every day to keep an area clutter free and clean, but in the long-run it will be worth it.

If you ever become overwhelmed, take a break and do something you enjoy

.

De-cluttering and cleaning is about making your home a much nicer place to live and helping you enjoy a less stressful life.

Spending less could be your golden ticket to financial freedom.

Before you go, I'd like to say "thank you" for purchasing my book.

I need to ask a favor, please take a moment and leave a review for this book where ever it was sold.

Word of mouth is my advertising.